ENERGY FOR THE FUTURE

NUCLEAR ENERGY

by Rachel Kehoe

WWW.FOCUSREADERS.COM

Focus Readers is distributed by North Star Editions:
sales@northstareditions.com | 888-417-0195

Produced for Focus Readers by Red Line Editorial.

Content Consultant: Xu Wu, Assistant Professor of Nuclear Engineering, North Carolina State University

Photographs ©: Shutterstock Images, cover, 1, 10, 15, 21, 22, 25, 26–27, 28; JPL-Caltech/NASA, 4–5; JPL-Caltech/MSSS/NASA, 7; US Air Force/AP Images, 8–9; Phil Degginger/Science Source, 12–13; SPL/Science Source, 17; Patrick Landmann/Science Source, 18–19

Library of Congress Cataloging-in-Publication Data
Library of Congress Cataloging-in-Publication Data is available on the Library of Congress website.

ISBN
978-1-63739-062-7 (hardcover)
978-1-63739-116-7 (paperback)
978-1-63739-219-5 (ebook pdf)
978-1-63739-170-9 (hosted ebook)

Printed in the United States of America
Mankato, MN
012022

ABOUT THE AUTHOR

Rachel Kehoe is a science writer and children's book author. She has published several articles about science and technology and enjoys researching climate change and sustainable energy sources. Rachel is a teacher who has lived in many countries around the world. She now calls Ontario, Canada, her home.

TABLE OF CONTENTS

CHAPTER 1

POWERING DISCOVERY

In August 2012, a rover named Curiosity landed on Mars. A rover is a wheeled robot that explores other planets. Curiosity is packed with tools for exploring. Its robotic arm has a camera, a drill, and a scoop. It can analyze rocks, drill into them, and collect the pieces. Computers inside the rover study the

Curiosity is the size of a small car and weighs 2,000 pounds (900 kg).

samples. All of these tests use a lot of power.

Previous Mars rovers used solar panels for energy. They needed lots of sunlight to work. During short winter days, the rovers couldn't work for long. Other times, dust storms blocked the sun's light. At these times, the rovers had no power at all. They couldn't move, use tools, or communicate with Earth.

To avoid these problems, Curiosity doesn't use solar power. Instead, it relies on a nuclear **generator**. Curiosity can work in dark and dusty locations. Nuclear energy supplies it with all the power it needs.

Curiosity has taken selfies on Mars with its robotic arm. This image does not show the arm holding the camera.

Curiosity was supposed to last for only two years. But as of 2021, it was still exploring Mars. Meanwhile, on Earth, nuclear energy powers many homes. It gives people light and heat. In the future, it will continue to be an important power source.

CHAPTER 2

THE HISTORY OF NUCLEAR ENERGY

Many discoveries led to nuclear energy. In 1896, a French scientist found that the metal uranium gives off energy. This energy is called **radiation**. It comes from inside **atoms**. Scientists later learned this energy can be dangerous. High levels can harm or kill living things. But scientists also learned how to use

Radiation sickness killed thousands of people after the atomic bombing of Japan in 1945.

radiation. In 1938, German scientists shot **neutrons** at a uranium atom. The atom split. It released energy as it broke. This process is called nuclear fission. Splitting one atom doesn't release much

INSIDE AN ATOM

All matter is made of tiny atoms. At the center of an atom is the nucleus. It is made up of protons and neutrons. Surrounding the nucleus are electrons.

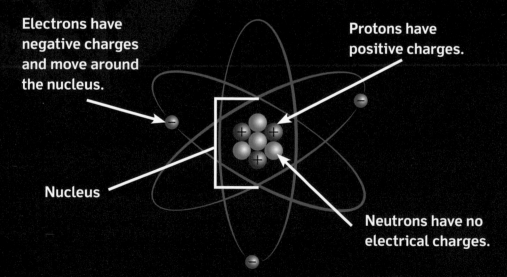

Electrons have negative charges and move around the nucleus.

Protons have positive charges.

Nucleus

Neutrons have no electrical charges.

energy. But splitting many at once does. In 1942, an Italian scientist managed to do just that.

In 1957, the United States built its first commercial **nuclear reactor**. It powered homes. By 2021, the United States had 94 reactors. They created nearly 20 percent of the country's electricity.

THE ATOMIC BOMB

Scientists created the atomic bomb during World War II (1939–1945). The bomb uses nuclear fission. In nuclear reactors, fission is controlled. But in the bomb, it is uncontrolled. In 1945, the United States dropped two atomic bombs on Japan. Hundreds of thousands of people died. The bombs showed the dangerous strength of uncontrolled fission.

CHAPTER 3

INSIDE THE REACTOR

Scientists need uranium for nuclear fission. Miners get the uranium from underground. Most natural uranium cannot be used for fission. So, scientists treat it with chemicals. They make U-235. This type of uranium is unstable. Its atoms will easily split apart.

Most natural uranium is U-238. Its atoms do not easily split apart.

Scientists form pellets with the uranium. The pellets go inside long metal rods. Stacks of rods form the center of a reactor. The rods are covered in water. Then scientists turn the reactor on. The U-235 atoms start to split. They release neutrons. The neutrons hit other U-235

NUCLEAR FUSION

Nuclear fusion is the opposite of fission. It involves crushing atoms together. This only happens under very high temperatures. The sun and other stars produce heat using nuclear fusion. The process creates vast amounts of energy. But it also takes a lot of energy to start the reaction. Several countries have built test nuclear-fusion reactors. As of 2021, nuclear fusion on Earth remained experimental.

Some nuclear reactors do not boil water. Instead, high-pressure conditions keep the water as a liquid.

atoms. Those atoms split, too. A chain reaction begins. Trillions of splits occur.

These splits create a huge amount of heat. The rods become hot. The water around them boils. It turns into steam. That steam spins the blades of a turbine. As this machine spins, it turns a generator. The generator creates electricity. The electricity travels across power lines. It goes to towns and homes.

Nuclear reactors are very powerful. Workers must monitor them. They make sure the reactors do not overheat. Water can help keep reactors cool. For this reason, reactors are built near lakes, rivers, and seas. That way, water is always available. Workers also use control rods. These rods take in neutrons. They can slow the pace of fission.

Sometimes there are emergencies. These include earthquakes and tsunamis. At these times, the whole system shuts down. Doing so protects workers and the reactor. In addition, reactors are built strong. Thick steel and concrete surround the core. Reactors are designed to contain the dangerous radiation.

BOILING WATER REACTOR

Unused steam is cooled in a condenser. The steam turns into liquid water, which is reused.

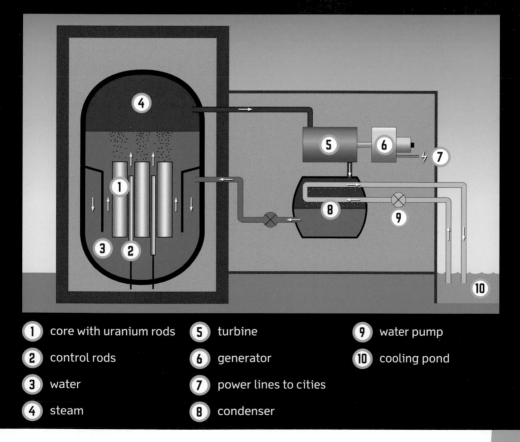

1	core with uranium rods	**5**	turbine	**9**	water pump
2	control rods	**6**	generator	**10**	cooling pond
3	water	**7**	power lines to cities		
4	steam	**8**	condenser		

CHAPTER 4

ADVANTAGES AND DISADVANTAGES

All energy sources have pros and cons. Today, people mainly use **fossil fuels**. These are nonrenewable resources. This means they will eventually run out. Uranium is also nonrenewable. Earth has enough of it to last nearly 100 years.

Still, nuclear power has many benefits. It can provide energy on a huge scale.

One tiny uranium pellet makes as much energy as 2,000 pounds (900 kg) of coal.

One small U-235 pellet makes as much energy as 149 gallons (564 L) of oil. And unlike fossil fuels, nuclear power makes clean energy. This means it does not contribute to **climate change**. Plus, it is a reliable source of energy. Power plants can run at full power all day and night.

Nuclear energy poses some drawbacks. Mining uranium releases gases that damage the **ozone layer**. Also, storing nuclear waste is a serious concern. After four to six years, the uranium inside a rod is spent. It will no longer produce a chain reaction. Workers remove spent fuel rods. But they can't throw the rods away. The rods contain radiation.

Nuclear waste is often sealed in huge metal drums.

Instead, workers place the rods in cooling pools. Water traps the radiation. The pools are sealed in thick concrete. Even cooled, the waste will give off radiation for thousands of years. So, it needs to be stored for a long time. Experts believe the waste should be

Hundreds of thousands of people fled Chernobyl after a nuclear explosion. The area is still mostly empty today.

stored deep underground. But some worry the waste could leak. People do not want the waste near their homes. For now, the waste is kept at nuclear plants. Some countries are studying how to recycle waste. They want to turn it into new fuel.

Nuclear energy can be dangerous in other ways. In 1986, an explosion occurred at the Chernobyl plant in Ukraine. The blast released huge amounts of radiation. Thousands died from the radiation's effects. Today, nuclear plants are made safer and stronger. Disasters are rare. But accidents still happen.

FUKUSHIMA DISASTER

In 2011, an earthquake hit Japan. A huge wave crashed into a nuclear power plant there. Water flooded the plant and knocked out safety systems. The fuel overheated, and backup cooling systems failed. Explosions released deadly radiation. People fled the nearby area. This disaster reminded the world of the risks of nuclear power.

POWERING MISSIONS

Nuclear reactors can power submarines. Just like on land, the reactors heat water to create steam. The steam drives the sub's propellers. This pushes the sub through the water. The sub can stay at sea for years without refueling.

The USS *Nautilus* was the first nuclear-powered sub. The US Navy built it in 1954. It set records for speed and distance underwater. It was also the first sub to travel under the North Pole. It traveled under ice caps for nearly 1,000 miles (1,600 km).

Nuclear reactors can power aircraft carriers, too. These ships serve as bases for aircraft. They carry fighter jets and more. The USS *Enterprise* was built in 1960. It logged 51 years of service.

The USS *Louisville* was active for 34 years before being decommissioned in 2021.

Nuclear energy also powers space missions. In 2004, the Cassini-Huygens spacecraft orbited Saturn. It sent back new information about the planet. The mission was so successful that it lasted until 2017. Nuclear power made it possible.

CHAPTER 5

THE FUTURE OF NUCLEAR ENERGY

By 2021, many nuclear plants were reaching the ends of their life spans. Building a nuclear plant takes years. It is also expensive. But the world needs clean energy sources. Fossil fuels will one day run out. They are also bad for the environment. Burning fossil fuels releases greenhouse gases. These gases trap heat

Coal power plants release greenhouse gases, which are warming the planet.

Some nuclear reactors have cooling towers. The towers do not give off pollution. They release steam.

in Earth's atmosphere. They are causing climate change.

In contrast, nuclear energy is clean. It could help many countries reduce their greenhouse gas emissions. In the United States, nuclear power is the largest source of clean energy. It produces the same amount of electricity as all renewable energy sources combined.

Researchers have begun to test new nuclear reactors. These reactors are cheaper. They are easier to build. And they are safer. Scientists continue to perfect nuclear energy. It can protect the climate. It is an energy for the future.

NUSCALE POWER MODULE

NuScale is a small reactor. It is 9 feet (2.7 m) across. It is 65 feet (20 m) tall. Its size makes it easy to build, move, and use. NuScale works inside a pool of water. The large pool contains the radiation. And if overheating occurs, the water will absorb the heat. This prevents the reactor from being damaged.

FOCUS ON
NUCLEAR ENERGY

Write your answers on a separate piece of paper.

1. Write a letter to a friend describing how a nuclear reactor works.

2. Do you think the benefits of nuclear power outweigh the risks? Why or why not?

3. How long will Earth's supply of uranium last?
    - **A.** a few years
    - **B.** 100 years
    - **C.** forever

4. What might happen if people started to use more nuclear energy instead of fossil fuels?
    - **A.** Greenhouse gas emissions would decrease.
    - **B.** Greenhouse gas emissions would increase.
    - **C.** Greenhouse gas emissions would stay the same.

Answer key on page 32.

GLOSSARY

atoms
The smallest building blocks of matter. They make up everything in the physical world.

climate change
A human-caused global crisis involving long-term changes in Earth's temperature and weather patterns.

fossil fuels
Energy sources that come from the remains of plants and animals that died long ago.

generator
A machine that turns the energy of motion into electricity.

neutrons
Tiny particles that have no electrical charge.

nuclear reactor
A device used to start and control a nuclear fission chain reaction. It is used at nuclear power plants to make electricity.

ozone layer
The part of Earth's atmosphere that takes in most of the sun's damaging rays, protecting Earth.

radiation
Energy in the form of waves or particles.

TO LEARN MORE

BOOKS

Burgan, Michael. *Chernobyl Explosion: How a Deadly Nuclear Accident Frightened the World*. North Mankato, MN: Capstone Publishing, 2018.

Doeden, Matt. *The Manhattan Project*. Minneapolis: Lerner Publications, 2019.

Smith-Llera, Danielle. *Mars Rover: How a Self-Portrait Captured the Power of Curiosity*. North Mankato, MN: Capstone Publishing, 2018.

NOTE TO EDUCATORS

Visit **www.focusreaders.com** to find lesson plans, activities, links, and other resources related to this title.

INDEX

Answer Key: 1. Answers will vary; **2.** Answers will vary; **3.** B; **4.** A

SNOW LEOPARDS